YOU ARE
MY DOGGO, AND
I AM YOUR PERSON

By Theresa Ann

Illustrated by Visoeale

ISBN 979-8-218-09779-0

Silent Books Publishing
silentbookspublishing.com

Silent Books Publishing is a self-publishing partnership company for aspiring and seasoned authors.

Dedicated to my grandchildren
I hope reading always takes you to new places

Hi! My name is Annie. I am a beagle. This story is about me and how I met my person, Nate.

Nate and I didn't always live together. I've lived in 3 different states!

My first mom got sick and couldn't take care of me.

When my mom went to a hospital, I had to stay with a foster mom. I was very sad to leave my mom. She was the only mom I knew. When I am sad, I whimper and have a long face.

My foster mom was a temporary mom. She kept me for a while but soon, I had to move to a new home. I had been in three foster homes.

Each time I moved, I had to get used to a new bed, a new routine, and a new family. Moving so much made me scared. When I am scared, I pee.
I pee on floors, beds, pillows, and shoes.

One day a nice mom-like person came to get me from my foster home and put me into a small crate. Just as moms do, she greeted me kindly, ruffled my fur, and smiled as she locked the crate. Then she carried me in the crate to a car, and we drove for many hours.

I felt so lonely in the crate. When I am lonely, I curl up in a ball and bury my nose in my blanket.

While I rode in the back of the car, the day turned to night. Finally, the door opened, and the mom-like person said, "We are here, Annie."

I was so worried! The fur on the back of my neck was standing up. I didn't understand what 'here' meant. I trembled. My tummy filled with butterflies, and my entire body shook and quivered.

The nice mom-like person put me down on the street. I was curious about where I was, but I could only see a home lit by a porch light. I used my nose to sniff everything in sight.

My nose led me to a young man and his mom, who seemed excited to see me! The young man bent down with a sweet smile, opened his palm, and let me sniff his hand. I was anxiously trembling because I was nervous about meeting new people.

In a soft voice, he said, "Hi, Annie. I'm Nate. We are going to take care of each other now. I'll be your person, and you can be my doggo." Nate ruffled my fur, and I nuzzled close to him as he said, "Annie, I think you feel broken, like me. We will be ok together." I still felt nervous about this new change, but I began to feel hopeful that I had found my forever home.

That night I slept with Nate in his apartment. He fed me dog food and treats and said soft, soothing words as he rubbed my belly. Nate told me why he needed me in between belly rubs. Nate had something that many people call addiction. Nate said we should call it substance use disorder.

Substance use disorder is a disease. Nate said it is when your brain and your body crave something that is not healthy for you. Nate had been sick for quite some time. He was sad, scared, lonely, and worried when he was sick. I understood Nate because I have felt those emotions too. That night, we both slept peacefully for the first time in a long time.

The next day, Nate and I took a long walk together. Nate said we could breathe fresh air and feel healthy when we walked. I like feeling healthy because I have so much energy! We would take these walks a couple of times each day.

Sometimes, Nate's mom, Gigi, would walk with us. On our walks, I chased squirrels and rabbits, and once I found a slice of pizza! I felt so happy that I had a giddy-up in my step!

Nate and I continued to care for each other every day.

In the evenings, Nate and I go for rides in his jeep. I ride in the front seat, Nate calls this shotgun, and I stick my head out the window and lick at the air. Sometimes we go to a drive-up store and get a pup cup. A special treat filled with ice cream just for me! After I eat my ice cream, my belly and heart feel full. I am thankful.

Sometimes I still get a little scared. When Nate goes to work, I miss him. I worry that I may lose this forever home.

I howl into the air to express my fear. When Nate comes home, he tells me he missed me, too. He rubs my belly to comfort me and says...

"I will always come back for you, Annie. You are my doggo, and I am your person."

This book was made possible in part due to the generous donation of others.
Seth Poling, who was diagnosed with ALS, will also benefit from this generosity.

Dr. Theresa Poling is a Family Nurse Practitioner, Associate Professor, Mom, Gigi, and Yogi. In her family practice clinic, she treats substance use disorder as a chronic disease. She sits on several prominent boards, and her life's purpose is to decrease barriers to care for those struggling with substance use disorder.